Constructing Gay Theology

Gay Men's Issues in Religious Studies Series,
Volume 2

Proceedings of the Gay Men's Issues in Religion
Consultation of the American Academy of Religion,
Fall 1989

Edited by
Michael L. Stemmeler
&
J. Michael Clark

Las Colinas
Monument Press
1991

Published by
Monument Press
P. O. Box 160361
Las Colinas, Texas 75016

Library of Congress Cataloging-in-Publication Data

Constructing gay theology / essays by J. Michael Clark ... [et al.]:
    edited by Michael L. Stemmeler & J. Michael Clark.
         p.   cm. -- (Gay men's issues in religious studies series ;
v. 2)
    "Proceedings of the Gay Men's Issues in Religion Consultation
of the American Academy of Religion, fall 1989"--Ser. t. p.
    Papers presented at the Annual Meeting of the American
Academy of Religion in Anaheim, Calif., 20 Nov 1989.
    Includes bibliographical references and index.
    ISBN 0-930383-19-2 : $7.00
    1. Homosexuality--Religious aspects--Christianity--Congresses.
2. Gay men--Religious life--Congresses. 3. Liberation theology--
Congresses. I. Clark, J. Michael (John Michael), 1953-   .
II. Stemmeler, Michael L., 1955-   . III. American Academy of
Religion. Gay Men's Issues in Religion Consultation. IV. American
Academy of Religion. Meeting (1989 : Anaheim, Calif.) V. Series.
BR115.H6C68   1991
261.8'35766--dc20   90-24987
                                                   CIP

Gay Men's Issues in Religious
Studies Series Review Committee

Forthcoming
in the
Gay Men's Issues in Religious Studies
Series:

Volume 3
Proceedings of the Gay Men's Issues
in Religion Group, American Academy of Religion,
Fall 1990, New Orleans

Gayspiritual

but

NonChristian

including papers by
Gary David Comstock,
Paul G. Schalow, &
Giovanni Vitiello,
with a response by
Jose I. Cabezon

* * *

Table of Contents

I. Michael L. Stemmeler

Introduction: A Call for Constructivity

After decades of defense against vicious social, political and religious attacks perpetrated against us by the nongay dominant society, gay men and lesbians have begun to realize that it is high time to affirm our own beings and identities in all areas of life. The affirmation of ourselves effects a direct challenge to the claims of social, political, and religious institutions to be the exclusive guardians of traditions and heritage(s) that should be accessible to all human beings. Gay men and lesbians have a rightful claim to these traditions--perhaps even more so than other population groups, by virtue of the fact that we have been effectively excluded for centuries from the enjoyment of the fruits of what is also *our* heritage. Since the validity of our claim has been established, what is needed now is the exercise of this rightful claim. Consequently, the contributions to this second volume of the *Gay Men's Issues in Religious Studies Series* are devoted to the problem of unapologetically constructing gay theology.[1]

Particularly in the vast field of religion--composed of the academic study of religion(s) just as much as of individual beliefs and collective religious practices--the articulation of the process of laying claim to a heritage and to traditions that are already our own is absolutely necessary. It is within religion that the myriad of petty denials and the many grave refusals of full recognition of gay men and lesbians in the social sphere have their roots. The following articles and the response to them, together address this problem from various angles.

Thomas M. Thurston's "Gay Theology of Liberation and the Hermeneutic Circle" is an attempt to analyze existing approaches toward a particularly gay liberation theology. His analysis follows the methodological lines of the hermeneutic circle offered by the Latin American liberation theologian Juan Luis Segundo. The rejection of both the mediating and the revisionist ethical positions of "making sense" of lived gay/lesbian existence leads Thurston to conclude that only an uninhibited affirmation of the very experience of gay men and lesbians bears sufficient grounds for a specific and undeniable gay theology.

J. Michael Clark's "Prophecy, Subjectivity, and Theodicy in Gay Theology: Developing a Constructive Methodology" sets the parameters for a gay theology. Clark emphasizes the just claim gay men and lesbians have to the religious traditions of which they are part, by right of birth. With reference to the major themes in the work of Carter Heyward, for example, he declares the prophetic *impetus* in gay liberation theology to be the element that has been developed from within the community. This *impetus* is therefore able to speak adequately about the experiences of gay men and lesbians. The prophetic *impetus* is also the element that empowers gay men and lesbians toward a radical critique of oppressive, necrophilic forces around us. The construction of gay theology depends on the affirmation of gay existence and experience as the foundation, and the prophetic denunciation of adversarial nongay religious and sociopolitical forces as the superstructure. Prophetic messages of liberation and critique, of the formation of communities on the margins of society, and of commitment to liberating *praxis* are part and parcel of methodological considerations.

E. Michael Gorman's "A Special Window: An Anthropological Perspective on Spirituality in Contemporary U.S. Gay Male Culture" thematizes the intricate relationship of religion and spirituality to other aspects of culture. The cultural environment created by gay men for their orientation and well-being serves as a symbolic universe. The metaphors of language employed by gay men in the description of significant events in their lives reveal a high degree of religious consciousness.

Enabled and catalyzed by the presence of the gay symbolic universe, the ritual of "coming out," for example, occupies the rank of a prime symbolic event, indispensable for the development of a mature gay self-consciousness. Gorman's final question asks how the gay symbolic universe relates to the experience of the divine. His answer develops out of the early Christian triad of proclamation, community, and service—a solution that has proven effective also in the context of Latin American liberation theology and within the feminist critique of patriarchally petrified religion and its institutions.

John J. McNeill's response emphasizes the importance of gay experience for the formulation of any gay theology, to which all three contributions witness. Validation of gay/lesbian existence cannot be furnished by outsiders. Any attempt to provide gay men and lesbians with a validation of their being that has not been generated from within will have to be met with a hermeneutics of suspicion. All too often, the real name of the game is co-optation rather than validation, even in the best of all possible attempts. McNeill is uncomfortable with Thurston's criticism that locates him within the revisionist camp of scholars who commit the hermeneutic crime of transposing contemporary ideas concerning sexuality into the world of Christian origins. Pointing toward the development of gay theology, McNeill proposes a reverse strategy that makes use of the traditional idea of the "discernment of spirits" and applies it to the interpretation of contemporary gay existence.

In the process of constructing gay theology, we again deal with a variant of *Exodus* theology. The ways of doing theology employed by the dominant culture(s) have left us dissatisfied. They advocate the denial of our experience, refuse us access to our traditions, and exclude our very being from full participation in our religious traditions. Constructing gay theology as self-*liberation* is also an act of self-*creation* as well as an act of creating the communities in which we live and serve.

The formation of new communities on the margins of society should not be interpreted as the establishments of "safe houses" for the despised, however. This would do nothing but cater to an ideology of forced ghettoization. Instead, new communities will have to emphasize the social component of our human lives that has to be nurtured by the experience of reciprocity and solidarity with their rejection of oppressive and exploitative structures. Such new communities will be centers of service to the physical and spiritual needs of their members and they will have to evolve into vantage points for the development of poignant critiques of exclusionary philosophies as well as of exclusionary sociopolitical and religious policies.

The liberating *indicatives* of the prophetic language component of gay liberation theology are augmented by liberating *imperatives* toward the establishment of genuine freedom for gay men and lesbians. This is the only way to allow us to live our gay and lesbian lives the way we want and have to live them. Whatever it is that gay experience and existence bring forth, it is *authentic* gay/lesbian experience and existence, because it is rooted in our lives. And, to that we raise our glasses.

11 October 1990,
on the third anniversary
of the 1987 March on Washington
for Lesbian & Gay Rights

---

[1]The articles included in this volume were originally presented at the second Gay Men's Issues in Religion Consultation within the American Academy of Religion (AAR), Anaheim, California, 20 November 1989. The present volume is *not* an official publication of the AAR.

II. Thomas M. Thurston

Gay Theology of Liberation and the Hermeneutic Circle

A theology of liberation can emerge when people of faith engage in religious reflection on their struggle for liberation. Lesbian/feminists such as Carter Heyward and Mary Hunt have already written works which speak to the lesbian struggle for liberation and could properly be called works of liberation theology. More commonly, however, their writings are grouped with other feminists rather than with other liberation theologians.[1] While gay men can support the work of feminists, especially lesbian/feminists, and while they ought to see how this struggle for justice relates to their own, they must not abdicate to others the responsibility for reflecting on the struggle for gay liberation. Feminist writings properly treat the needs of women; we must not expect them to speak fully to the needs of gay men. Keeping in mind the significant overlap between gay men's and lesbians' struggle for liberation and the many ways in which our goals are the same, nevertheless gay men must look to themselves rather than to their lesbian sisters or their nongay sympathizers for a gay theology of liberation.

Liberation theology itself finds its roots in the Latin American struggle for liberation and the theologians who are spokespeople for that movement. Often these theologians studied under European political theologians and their early writings resembled those of their teachers. And yet, the liberation theologians distinguish themselves from the political theologians by pointing out their own direct involvement in the struggle for liberation. Political theologians, they point out, write about *someone else's* liberation.

Those gay men who are participating in their own liberation and yet who have chosen to remain involved with the church have too often been content to let others advance their cause. Theologians who have addressed the religious concerns of gay men are most often progressive nongay moral theologians. These theologians do not speak of "gay people" at all, but speak about the morality of "homosexual acts."[2] While they concede that homosexuals may have sex in good conscience if they mimic heterosexual marriage, this admission does not address broader issues of gay/lesbian liberation. Gay men ought properly to ask church leaders why Christianity has been so strongly focused on sexual issues throughout its history. We ought also to question a theology which allowed the burning of sodomites and witches. We want to know why homophobia and gay-bashing so strongly correlate with frequent churchgoing. The issue of sexual ethics, therefore, is only a minor part of a gay theology of liberation.

The issue for a gay theology of liberation, then, is "Why are gay people oppressed and how does the gospel speak to their liberation?" James Cone, in discussing Black theology, has expressed the relationship between theology and the struggle for liberation: "Theology's sole reason for existing is to put ordered speech to the meaning of God's activity in the world, so that the community of the oppressed will recognize that their inner thrust for liberation is not only consistent with the gospel but is the gospel of Jesus Christ."[3]

The French Canadian Guy Menard suggests that Juan Luis Segundo's hermeneutic circle be adopted as a methodological guide in developing a gay theology of liberation.[4] Segundo's work, *The Liberation of Theology*, is still the *locus classicus* for method in liberation theology. Segundo suggests that certain attempts at liberation theology fall short of their goal and are not really liberating. By following Segundo's guidelines, we may criticize previous efforts at doing theology from a gay perspective. Furthermore, using Segundo's method can help to assure us that our theology is indeed about liberation, and not merely a revisionist project.

Segundo's starting point for the discussion of method is the hermeneutic circle. "Hermeneutics" means a method of interpreting a text and, in this case, interpreting the bible. Segundo's hermeneutic circle is the continuing change in our interpretation of the bible, which is dictated by continuing changes in our present-day reality, both individual and social. Segundo notes that the term "hermeneutic circle" goes back to Rudolf Bultmann, but claims both a more expanded and a more appropriate use of the term.[5]

Two prior conditions must be met in order to have a hermeneutic circle. First, the questions rising out of the present must be rich enough and general enough to force a change in our contemporary conceptions of life, death, knowledge, society, politics, and the world in general. At the very least, there must be a pervasive suspicion about our ideas and value judgments. These questions and suspicions force theology to come back to reality and to ask itself new and decisive questions. The second prior condition for Segundo's hermeneutic circle is that if theology assumes it can respond to the new questions without changing its customary interpretation of scriptures, this immediately ends the hermeneutic circle.[6] Before examining the specific steps of the hermeneutic circle, let us first see if gay/lesbian experience fulfills these two preconditions.

Certainly the problems posed to theology by gay/lesbian experience are rich enough to direct us toward the hermeneutic circle. Gay people pose questions which the contemporary theological discussion is unable to deal with. The contemporary discussion reduces its treatment of gay people to a discussion of homosexuality. The discussion of homosexuality is reduced to sexual ethics and sexual ethics to a discussion of genital acts. Being gay (or lesbian) is also a social identity. The homosexual began to emerge from the shadows of sexual conformity to become a distinct personality in the nineteenth century. Even the earliest spokespeople for what was to become gay sensibility--such as Walt Whitman, John Addington Symonds, and Edward Carpenter--saw homosexuality related to a nobility of spirit, an ethos, a vision of a society of equals. Karl Heinrich Ulrichs, perhaps the first activist for the rights of homosexuals, and Magnus Hirschfeld, founder of the first organization for advancing the rights of homosexual people, resisted political and scientific systems which justified the oppression of homosexuals. Harry Hay, founder of the Mattachine Society in the 1950s, saw the possibility of a highly ethical homosexual culture.

Today, a very extensive and fully developed gay subculture exists, whose existence does not depend on procreation or the nuclear family with its underlying mores. This subculture challenges the dominant society's views of life, death, gender, sex, family, relationships, and so forth. A theology which focuses narrowly on the physical configurations of two people who share a bed and which refuses to recognize the challenge of gay/lesbian culture speaks neither to gay people nor for them. Thus, gay/lesbian experience meets the first precondition of the hermeneutic circle. A new situation has clearly rendered traditional assumptions obsolete.

Little argument is required to show that a gay theology of liberation cannot be accommodated to the customary interpretation of scriptures, the second precondition. No amount of exegetical contortions can overcome the fact that sex between men is condemned in both testaments and lesbian sex is condemned in Paul's epistle to the Romans. Yet, this fact does not halt theological argument. Just as gay men and lesbians cannot explain away the biblical condemnations of homosexual acts, no manipulations by abolitionists could remove the bible's tolerance for slavery, nor can the political liberationists take away the bible's demand for obedience to authority, nor the feminists the subordination of women. Yet, there comes a point in the unfolding of God's good news in history when people say: These words are words of oppression, they are not the gospel, they are not from God. A new reading of scripture is necessary in which these oppressive passages do not obscure the gospel.

If a situation meets the preconditions for moving through the hermeneutic circle, as we have now seen that gay/lesbian experience does, Segundo suggests that one may proceed through the circle along four decisive steps:

> **1.** Our new way of experiencing reality leads us to ideological suspicion.
> **2.** We apply our ideological suspicion to the ideological superstructure in general and to theology in particular.
> **3.** Our new way of experiencing reality leads to exegetical suspicion that the prevailing interpretation of scripture has not taken important pieces of data into account.
> **4.** Consequently, a new hermeneutic emerges--that is, a new way of interpreting the fountainhead of faith, the scriptures.[7]

The first step--*ideological suspicion*--has long been underway. From Symonds and Ulrichs onward, gay men and lesbians have suspected that the ideology which oppresses and marginalizes homosexuals is false. In the 1960s homophile groups such as the Mattachine Society under the leadership of Frank Kameny confronted the guardians of that ideology, the mental health community. The American Psychiatric Association's decision to remove homosexuality from its list of mental illnesses in 1973 was as much the result of political and ideological struggle as it was of scientific advancement. Ronald Bayer documents this struggle in his book, *Homosexuality and American Psychiatry: The Politics of Diagnosis.*[8] The ideological struggle continues today through such organizations as the National Gay Rights Advocates, the National Gay and Lesbian Task Force, the Lambda Legal Defense Fund and the Human Rights Campaign Fund.

The second step along the hermeneutic circle requires a move from the suspicion of ideology to a critique, especially a critique of theology. Gay people have been slow to develop this *theological critique.* One reason for this is that a large percentage of gay men and lesbians have exercised their suspicion of theology by leaving the church when they left the closet. Perhaps the best expression of suspicion from within the Roman Catholic Church is *Homosexuality and Social Justice,* a 1982 report by the Task Force on Gay/Lesbian Issues of the Archdiocese of San Francisco.[9] The Task Force, which was instigated to address the problem of antigay violence, found that attackers were often young, Hispanic, and Catholic. They concluded that the issue of violence against gay men and lesbians could not be addressed independently of the ideology which supports a negative attitude toward them, *viz.* the teachings of the Catholic Church on homosexuality. Not surprisingly, the archdiocese rejected the report. Liberation is more often the result of struggle from below than benevolence from above.

When moral theologians writing on homosexuality have exercised a suspicion of theology, they have moved from what Charles Curran calls the mediating position to a revisionist position.[10] The mediating position is exemplified by such theologians as Curran and Philip Keane who, while not challenging the traditional position of the Catholic Church on homosexuality, develop a theological position which will accommodate homosexuals within the church by way of exception and out of pastoral concern.

Both Keane and Curran see heterosexuality as normative. According to Keane, homosexual acts always involve a significant degree of ontic evil because they lack openness to procreation and the man/woman relationship as it functions in marriage. Yet, they do not necessarily become morally evil because under certain circumstances there may be a truly proportionate justification for them.[11]

Charles Curran places the discussion of homosexuality within the context of sinful human nature after the fall. Thus, the heterosexual relationship is part of the ideal natural order. Human realities such as self-defense, the just war, slavery, and private property have to do with human nature after the fall. Similarly, Curran maintains that homosexuality exists only as a result of the fall, and that homosexuals have a different psychic structure, and therefore a different sexuality. As an accommodation to this reality, Curran maintains that "for an irreversible or constitutional homosexual, homosexual acts in the context of a loving relationship striving for permanency can be and are morally good."[12]

Both of these theologians see how the traditional theological position is oppressive to gay men and lesbians, but are unwilling to challenge the authority of that tradition. They accept individual homosexuals while supporting the system that calls homosexuality "sick." They do not reflect on the significance of gay/lesbian culture at all. Thus, they are unable to move to the third step of the hermeneutic circle, *suspicion of scripture* based on a new situation.

On the other hand, proponents of the revisionist position suspect that the traditional position, as presently articulated, does not reflect an accurate reading of Christian sources and Christian history. Yet, within the revisionist camp, the level of suspicion in John McNeill, John Boswell, and Tom Horner, for example, differs from the level in Robin Scroggs and George Edwards. The former do not realize that their suspicions arise from a new way of experiencing the world. Anachronistically, they project contemporary experience back into Christian origins, imposing the category of sexual orientation on ancient texts.

McNeill and Boswell reach generally the same conclusions in their treatment of the bible. McNeill maintains that the only homosexual acts clearly condemned in scripture are

those engaged in by otherwise truly heterosexual individuals as an expression of contempt or
self-centered lust and are usually associated
with some form of idol worship.[13] Boswell
does not overturn the condemnation of homosexual relations in Leviticus. Instead, he
maintains that this passage is irrelevant for
Christians, who did not otherwise accept leviti-
cal regulations within Christian moral law.[14]
With this stance, Christians should accept homosexuals until new biblical exegesis over-
turns this position.[15]

As an historian, Boswell refrains from
developing an explicit position on homosexuality and ethics. McNeill, finding no explicit
condemnation of homosexual relations in the
bible, maintains that the same moral rules ap-
ply to homosexuals as to heterosexuals. He
maintains that, "those [sexual acts] that are responsible, respectful, loving, and truly promo-
tive of the good of both parties are moral; those
that are exploitative, irresponsible, disrespect-
ful, or destructive of the true good of either
party must be judged immoral."[16] While this
position is progressive and perhaps helpful, it
does not begin to touch on the history of oppression that sexual nonconformists have experienced at the hands of the church. It does
not give us many resources in our struggle for
liberation.

On the other hand, Scroggs and Edwards realize that there is a *new situation,*
thereby completing the third step. Yet, neither

proceeds to complete the hermeneutic circle. Scroggs maintains that the new situation is that contemporary homosexual relationships are mutual, caring relationships between adults. Thus, he affirms Paul's condemnation of Hellenistic pederasty. Furthermore, he takes no stand on whether Paul would have condemned contemporary homosexual relationships.[17] But, Edwards proceeds to the third step in the hermeneutic circle. He criticizes Paul's heterosexism just as the feminists criticize Paul's patriarchy.[18] Yet, when he develops his own position on sexual ethics, he does not use a hermeneutic that proceeds from gay/lesbian experience, but imposes a heterosexual standard, albeit a fairly progressive one. Edwards states that "the assumption of this treatment of the future of sexuality is that the relation of homosexuality to *agape* is no different in principle than that of heterosexuality."[19] He stops short of the fourth step of the hermeneutic circle.

Menard self-consciously uses Segundo's method in exploring the pathway for a gay theology of liberation. After reviewing the treatment of homosexual acts in scripture and Christian tradition, he comments that only the development of the modern human sciences could furnish the conditions for a radical reexamination of the homosexual question.[20] Thus, for Menard the real liberators of homosexuals are the human sciences--not gay men and lesbians themselves. Bayer's study may not have been available to him at the time of his writing, since Menard does not suspect the extent to which the gay/lesbian rights movement created the conditions for the human sciences to view homosexuality more positively. Menard's claims notwithstanding, the new situation does not come from the human sciences allowing gay people to experience homosexuality differently. On the contrary, gay people have forced the human sciences to view homosexuality differently.

Despite his curious route, Menard crystallizes an important element of the fourth step of the hermeneutic circle--*readings of scripture based on a hermeneutic that arises from gay/lesbian experience.* These readings are not just isolated words or passages of limited significance, but expressions of the central message of salvation.

One such reading focuses on the New Testament revolution. The Hebrew Bible considered certain people irrevocably condemned. Among these were men who engaged in homosexual acts. Yet, the mission of Jesus reached out to those placed on the margins of society--sinners, lepers, children, adulterous women, heretics, Samaritans, tax collectors, or simply people of little importance. Jesus gives radical expression to the heart of the biblical tradition, doing works of a God who loves the widows and orphans, a God who commands the Jews to feed the stranger, since the Jews were once strangers in Egypt (cf., Deut. 10:18). This same theme was a constant theme of the prophets, who took the attitude toward the outsider as an index of Israel's conformity to justice and the love of God. Deuteronomy reminds Israel that it owes its liberation to God, since the Jews were once strangers in Egypt.

Sexual minorities are also among those outsiders brought in by what Menard calls the New Testament Revolution. In Deuteronomy 23:1-2, eunuchs and bastards are excluded from the assembly of the Lord. Yet, Isaiah 56:4-6 envisions the day when eunuchs will enter the temple and receive an everlasting name. Indeed, the author of the Acts of the Apostles records for all time the story of the eunuch servant of the queen of Ethiopia who accepted the gospel, was baptized, and was filled with the Holy Spirit (Acts 8:28-39). We need not argue here that the eunuch engaged in homosexual acts, as some have.[21] More significant is that his impaired sexual status put him outside the ordinary pattern of family and procreation, like the childless widow, and placed him in a position considered accursed by God. The dynamic of the reign of God runs contrary to what people commonly regard as blessing or curse. In this dynamic gay men and lesbians see God's special solicitude for themselves--as oppressed people on the margins of society. Acceptance of them and other excluded and oppressed people is an index of the churches' conformity to the love of God.[22]

I suggested earlier that attempts at a gay theology of liberation have been incomplete because they have erred in their attempt(s) to

name the new hermeneutical situation. All
have tried to find something *outside* gay and
lesbian experience which they can use to validate gay and lesbian experience. However,
Gustavo Gutierrez warns us against putting
theory before practice in the project of liberation. The oppressed do not *need* any outside
confirmation to know that their oppression is
wrong. The pre-theological moment which
brings about the new theological reality is not
some theoretical advance, but the actual
struggle for liberation. As Gutierrez pointed
out, theology rises only at sundown. Theology
does not produce pastoral activity; it reflects
upon it. Theology must find in pastoral activity the presence of the spirit inspiring the action of the Christian community. This activity
--real, committed service to others--must come
first. Theology follows; it is a second step.[23]

The reason, then, that there is a new hermeneutical situation for speaking about gay
people and gay/lesbian relationships is not because they are now mutual, while previously
they were exploitative; not because they are
now between people of roughly the same age,
while previously they were pederastic; and,
certainly not because the medical establishment no longer calls homosexuality an illness,
while previously it did. The new situation was
brought about by the struggles of gay men and
lesbians. These struggles came to full flower
twenty plus years ago with the Stonewall Re-
bellion and its aftermath. The homophile

movement in this country since World War II laid the foundations and set the conditions of possibility for this flowering. The result is that for the first time since the classical period of Greece, people in same-sex relationships are publicly demanding that our relationships be recognized as praiseworthy and right. Whereas previously we were all too inclined to accept society's evaluation of ourselves, to seek therapy from the doctors and absolution from the priests, today we validate our own experience, telling the doctors that our homosexuality does not make us sick and telling the priests that it does not make us sinners.

The struggle for gay/lesbian liberation, then, expresses the *ideological suspicion* of gay people. I suggest that *theological suspicion,* the second step in the hermeneutic circle, may be exercised through a suspicion of the church's treatment of sexuality in general. Christian sexual theology was solidified in the late Roman Empire, when Christianity came to dominate society. Sexual theology grew out of an understanding of the human being as a rational animal, the human essence therefore being rationality. Sexual activity detracted from rationality and, therefore, was always suspect, although sex was allowable for its rational purpose--procreation. At that time Christianity was closely identified with asceticism. Complete sexual continence within the celibate state was certainly seen as the most noble choice of life styles. The problem is that this view of the person is no longer widely accepted. Yet, especially within the Roman Church, the theology based on this anthropology still has a wide influence—for example on the requirement of priestly celibacy, on the policy regarding birth control, on the policy regarding homosexuality, and, most tragically, on the policy on AIDS education.

The *new theological reality*, step three of the hermeneutic circle, can be summarized by the 1968 statement by the North American Coalition of Homophile Organizations (NACHO)—*gay is good!* The statement takes a more theological form in Dignity's statement of Position and Purpose. Here Dignity affirms that "our gay and lesbian sexuality can be expressed in a manner consonant with Christ's teachings."[24] Dignity itself, an association of gay and lesbian Catholics and their families and friends, is a continuing expression of this insight. Yet, Dignity has done little on an organizational or written level to develop this insight into a gay hermeneutic. Nevertheless, the NACHO and Dignity statements are of insurmountable significance because they are landmark statements by gay men and lesbians expressing the truth of our lives to a society and/or a church which hitherto have refused to listen to our experience.

Reinterpreting the fountainhead of faith, step four of the hermeneutic circle, is more than a lifetime project. Those who undertake this project assume the legitimacy of gay/les-

bian experience. They will articulate what
Menard calls the New Testament revolution
and will help show gay men and lesbians that
our struggle for liberation is the very gospel of
Jesus Christ.

---

[1]cf., Carter Heyward, "Heterosexist theology:
Being above it all," *Journal of feminist studies in religion*
3.1(Spring 1987), pp. 29-38; *The redemption of God: A theology of mutual relation* (New York: Univ. Press of America, 1982); and, *Touching our strength: The erotic as power
and the love of God* (San Francisco: Harper & Row, 1989).

[2]The terms "gay," "homosexual," and "homosexual acts" herein require some comment. "Gay" and
"homosexual" both have to do with identity and are social constructs. "Gay" is a social identity. By gay I mean
those homosexual or bisexual men who accept that label
for themselves and who are in some way involved with
that public subculture which in this country reached a
watershed in the gay/lesbian liberation movement of
the late 1960s. A homosexual is a person who has an
abiding sexual and affectional attraction to persons of
his/her own sex. Homosexual acts are sexual acts between people of the same sex. With these definitions
"homosexual" is more encompassing than "gay," but
only gay people engage in a gay theology of liberation.
A theology of liberation is a religious reflection on one's
struggle for liberation, an experience which those in the
closet do not have. The term "homosexual acts" has a
ring of objectivity which pretends to transcend social
constructions. It reflects the tendency, especially in Roman Catholic theology, to evaluate sexual activity based

on physical rather than subjective criteria. Yet, it is more subjective than the earlier term, "sodomy," which could also refer to anal intercourse between husband and wife. The idea of setting up one category of nonreproductive sexual acts for special consideration becomes more significant after the churches start condoning other forms of nonreproductive sex.

[3]James H. Cone, *A black theology of liberation* (Philadelphia: Lippincott, 1970), p. 17, as cited in: Juan Luis Segundo, *The liberation of theology,* J. Drury, trans. (Maryknoll, NY: Orbis Books, 1975, 1976), p. 26.

[4]Guy Menard, *De Sodom a l'Exode: Jalons pour une theologie de la liberation gaie* (Laval, Quebec: Guy St-Jean, 1982), p. 43.

[5]Segundo, p. 8.

[6]*Ibid.,* pp. 8-9.

[7]*Ibid.,* p. 9.

[8]Ronald Bayer, *Homosexuality and American psychiatry: The politics of diagnosis* (New York: Basic Books, 1981).

[9]Task Force on Gay/Lesbian Issues, *Homosexuality and social justice* (San Francisco: Consultation on Homosexuality, Social Justice, and Roman Catholic theology, 1982, 1986).

[10]Charles E. Curran, *Transition and tradition in moral theology* (Notre Dame: Univ. Notre Dame Press, 1979), p. 69.

[11]Philip S. Keane, *Sexual morality: A Catholic perspective* (New York: Paulist Press, 1977), pp. 71-91.

[12]Curran, pp. 71-74.

[13]John J. McNeill, *The church and the homosexual* (Boston: Beacon Press, 1976, 1988), pp. 53-56, 65-66.

[14]John Boswell, *Christianity, social tolerance, and homosexuality* (Chicago: Univ. Chicago Press, 1980), pp. 107-113.

[15]A most convincing attack on Boswell's position is Richard B. Hays, "Relations natural and unnatural: A response to John Boswell's exegesis of Romans I," *Journal of religious ethics* 14.1(Spring 1986), pp. 184-215. Hays shows that Boswell has an interior contradiction in the way he applies his essentialist assumptions.

[16]McNeill, p. 32.

[17]Robin Scroggs, *The New Testament and homosexuality* (Philadelphia: Fortress Press, 1983), pp. 126-128.

[18]George R. Edwards, *Gay/lesbian liberation: A biblical perspective* (New York: Pilgrim Press, 1984), p. 99.

[19]*Ibid.*, p. 113.

[20]Menard, p. 107.

[21]cf., Tom Horner, *Jonathan loved David: Homosexuality in biblical times* (Philadelphia: Westminster Press, 1978), pp. 101, 124.

[22]Menard, pp. 185-189.

[23]Gustavo Gutierrez, *A theology of liberation*, C. Inda & J. Eagleson, trans. (New York: Orbis Books, 1971, 1973, 1988), p. 9.

[24]cited in: Dignity Task Force on Sexual Ethics, *Pastoral letter on sexual ethics: A preliminary study document* (Washington: Dignity, 1987), 11.29-30.

III. J. Michael Clark

Prophecy, Subjectivity, and Theodicy in Gay Theology: Developing a Constructive Methodology

After two decades of contemporary gay liberation, gay men and lesbians have become aware that the seemingly endless arguments to justify gay and lesbian existence with biblical exegesis and to achieve ordination in traditional denominations have together become a Kafkaesque drain upon our energies. The institutional religious system clearly functions so as to diffuse our efforts, keeping us waiting and negotiating for a positive response which is unlikely ever to come. Rather than expending our energies in such futile pursuits, gay men and lesbians need, instead, to lay an assertive and righteous claim upon the religious traditions and heritage into which we were born. Gay men and lesbians need henceforth to find in ourselves "the courage and audacity to create our own theology,"[1] to speak theologically *as gay people*, rather than continuing to acquiesce, to accept, and therefore passively to endorse our exclusion from religious, spiritual, and theological activities. Gay people must make a commitment to be a force to be reckoned with in theology by claiming and assuming our right to theologize and to speak prophetically.

Gay liberation theology will necessarily be prophetic--using our position at the very edge of our religious heritage as our standpoint for interpreting and speaking both to and from our tradition. It entails standing forthrightly as much in judgment upon our heritage as informed by that heritage. In developing a feminist theology, for example, Rosemary Ruether has described a dilemma which gay theology also shares: "On the one hand, we must confront the fact that scripture and theology have contributed to these very evils that trouble us. They have functioned as sanctions of evil. Yet, we discover within [them] essential resources to unmask these very failures of religion."[2] While Judaism and Christianity have unabashedly sanctioned the evils of homophobia and even gay genocide--for, in the popular consciousness, at least, no contextual exegesis can undo either Leviticus' demand for death to homosexual men or Romans' vehement homophobia--that same two-prong tradition also carries the criterion for self-criticism-- the prophetic demand for justice.

Working prophetically with George Edwards, for example, gay theology will reject

that side of the western religious heritage
which worships a judgmental God "who des-
ignates homosexuals as objects of divine
anger," at once realizing the oppression which
such "divine wrath" entails and rejecting the
"misdirected moral condemnation" which is er-
roneously derived from this judgmental image
of God.[3] Gay theology will prophetically insist
that injustice and homophobia, *not* sexuality,
draw divine judgment. Gay theology will recognize that "theology must be done, [and] can
only be done, by those who situate themselves
in the reality of oppression, and whose theology is a reflection of liberating praxis."[4] In
other words, gay liberation theology can only
be done at the margins, by those who refuse
tokenism and assimilation, by those who par-
ticipate in the sociopolitical tasks and goals of
gay liberation, by those who, unashamed,
share in the subcultural and frequently ghet-
toized life of openly gay men and lesbians and,
at the same time, by those whose memory of
their own closets informs both their theology
and praxis with compassion for those who
cannot yet "embrace their exile."[5] Gay liberation theology must be an assertive and even
defiant celebration of life and a reconstruction
of theology—at the margins.

Both the assumption of a prophetic
function for gay theology and the relationship
of gay theology (and individual gay and lesbian theologians) to the Judaeo-Christian heritage further entail two other qualifiers for

such theological activity. Gay theology must be focused upon the here and now, the particularities of this time and place for gay people --not only in the subjective experience of gay people both collectively and individually, but also in the subjectivity of each gay or lesbian theologian's perceptions of, participation in, and interpretation of gay and lesbian life. Indeed, theology for us must be focused not upon heaven, but upon earth, always pointing toward the horizontality of God in our midst, a God dependent upon human justice-seeking and -making to be manifest. As Carter Heyward has said, theology is not "about God as God is in Godself, but rather about us as we experience God in this world at this time among ourselves."[6] Our theological activity becomes grounded in our human subjectivity, as Richard Rubenstein has described when he says,

> ...The ultimate relevance of theology is anthropological. Though theology purports to make statements about God, its significance rests on what it reveals about the theologian. ...All theologies are inherently subjective. They are statements about the way in which the theologian experiences [the] world.[7]

This methodological standpoint also means, then, that gay theology depends heavily upon the individual theologian; it derives, for example, from what *I* come to believe, based upon and informed by *my* sources and *my* experience and interpretation of gay life, for which *I* alone, and not those sources, am ultimately responsible. Doing and writing gay theology becomes a dialogue of and about *personal* understandings, in order for us to discover commonalities and to celebrate differences. Our theologizing is thus provisional and tentative, as well as dynamic and never authoritatively complete or "once-and-for-all." Our theology, as an ongoing activity, must exist in the "morally ongoing openness" of mutuality, reciprocity, and dialogue.[8] It indeed aspires to be the communication of an "inner world," or perspective upon the world, which the theologian "suspects others may share."[9] Carter Heyward elaborates when she says,

> ...Good constructive theology is done in the praxis of concrete situations, in which the doers of theology speak for and about themselves, rather than for and about others or humanity in general by attempting to universalize their experiences of what is true or good.
>
> ...This means ... that theology must be done modestly, in recognition that all theological images and patterns are limited—in terms of truth and intelligibility—by the boundaries of the life experiences of those who construct them.[10]

Our modest particularity and our provisional sharing of gay theology *as an activity* can ideally help us, therefore, to avoid projecting any of our work upon another as "universally" true.

If indeed, "the vision of the theologian is affected by the particularities of his or her experience,"[11] then I must acknowledge, up front, all the particularities of my past, my upbringing, my training, my gender, my economic standing, and my race. For if my theological activity and reflection have any broader, dialogical value for us as gay people, it will come through acknowledging my particularity, and not from failing to confront my "presuppositions." In so exploring and elucidating each individual's subjectivity, gay liberation theology also acquires a confessional quality which must necessarily undergird the modesty of our provisional assertions. My own gay being, for example, is not just a matter of what I do in bed with my lover, but my own particular way of perceiving, interpreting, interacting, and being in the world. It is my standpoint for defiantly creating wholeness or integretous personal unity out of paradox, conflict, and even rejection, as well as for doing theology. My own experience of gay life and gay oppression is the particular web or nexus of being--of personal subjectivity--from within which I can begin to shape understandings of God, of people, and of the divine/human relationship, however provisional and partial those may be.

This emphasis on subjectivity must not, however, emerge without a context, without

qualification. Rosemary Ruether reminds both
feminist and gay/lesbian theologians that we
cannot rely on mere subjectivity; we require
grounding in an "historical community and
tradition" for our prophecy to be authentic
criticism.[12] As a result, as gay people we are
brought back to our rootedness at the fringes
of our tradition. We are called to synthesize
our gay and lesbian being with an often homophobic and yet equally justice-seeking tradition, and in the process of effecting that synthesis, to derive the critical principles for our
theology. Among those criteria will be an in-
sistence upon the right of gay men and lesbians to full humanity--spiritually, socially,
politically, and medically. Malcolm Boyd, for
example, has insisted that "our spiritual needs
cry out to be met, honestly and fully, [and to
be] integrated with our sexual and other
needs."[13] Our theology will thus seek to nurture full humanity or wholeness, for gay
people and ultimately for *all* people, by reinte-
grating sexuality and spirituality with full, un-
hindered participation in social existence,
while nevertheless remaining critical of the
status quo. It will in turn also affirm and celebrate the particularity and difference of genuine pluralism and reject *ex*clusivity, seeking
instead an *in*clusivity of all genders, classes,
and races, and sharing with Ruether the belief
that "any principle of religion or society that
marginalizes one group of persons as less than
fully human diminishes us all."[14]

Our theology will thus remain "anthropological," connected with the actual life of our people and of other people, accounting for and not dismissing the negatives of historical existence--both sociologically and biologically-- while simultaneously affirming the intrinsic value of life in itself, apart from any supernatural validation. We will accept the limits of God whereby God is not a *deus ex machina* and thereby take seriously our human responsibility for creating justice. Our realism, however, will lead us not into despair or to waiting for rescue, but rather to an empowered ability to fuse our ideas with participation in the tasks and processes of change, toward a synthesis of theology and praxis, or, as Carter Heyward has described it, toward a "theology and ministry of *radical participation.*"[15]

Taking seriously our historical and biological life and its limitations, as well as taking seriously both the limits of divine power to rescue us and thus our responsibility for action, also means our gay theology will not ignore AIDS, tragedy, or death. No gay theology will hold our attention, much less our respect, unless it confronts both homophobic violence and AIDS. In fact, we may actually discover in our very experiences of seeming godforsakenness--whether in incidences of human injustice or in the absence of divine rescue from AIDS--a strange empowerment and therein God's compassionate companionship on behalf of the victims of oppression and tragedy. God's intimacy with us can enable us to forgive divine limitations, to develop compassion for one another, and to claim in our depths the spiritual resources for appropriate responsibility for shaping our own lives, for seeking social change, and for caring for those who are suffering from AIDS. Our refusal to succumb to despair and our facing the future, in spite of homophobia and even AIDS, in "radical participation," becomes the corporate gay and lesbian embodiment of our synthesis of theology and praxis.[16]

Methodological considerations of the provisional nature of gay theology thus far include a rejection of apologetics and of requiring outside authority or validation, in exchange for an assertive, prophetic role at the margins of Judaeo-Christianity. Gay theology shifts the focus from the vertical to the horizontal, to the here and now particularities of gay men and lesbians and of God's presence on our behalf. It fuses subjectivity with a grounding in both gay and lesbian life and in the justice-seeking side of our heritage. It moves toward a wholism of humanity, and of gay and lesbian humanity, and does not flinch from the realities of either human injustice or divine limitations in our present experience; it exhorts us to assume responsibility for active participation in our community and in the world. Consistent across this range of ideas is an absence of reliance upon scriptural or ecclesiastical authorities and, instead, an assump-

tion about the value of gay and lesbian experience as the grounding for our theology-as-dia-
logue.

Our experience as gay and lesbian
people in a predominantly homophobic western culture and ethos is in fact the present locus of, and ultimately the primary source for,
our particular liberation theology. And once
again, the work of certain feminist theologians
can be understood as equally paradigmatic for
gay theology. Feminist theology has essentially recovered and revalued human experience, and particularly the experience of oppressed and marginalized peoples, as a legitimate norm for appraising and evaluating theology and as an acceptable standpoint or
source for critically (re)constructing theology.
As a result, religious tradition mediated by
scripture and church doctrine or dogma can
now take a "back seat," informing theological
work as a valuable resource, but as one no
longer holding any oppressively binding authority over us. Theologizing now becomes
grounded in "a realization of our experience
[and] the capacity to be aware of, and to reflect
upon, the experience of being human."[17]
Specifically, minority experience and story becomes *the* norm for doing prophetic liberation
theology, as theology and praxis are insepara-
bly fused.

This fusion of experience with theoretical reflections upon God's presence with, or
advocacy on behalf of, the oppressed utterly

recasts theology. Sheila Collins goes so far as to say that "*nothing* that is of us can be alien to our theology."[18] Carter Heyward follows this same line of thought when she suggests both that theology is "the capacity to discern God's presence here and now and to reflect on what that means" and that the effectiveness of our theological reflections "rests on the extent to which we understand and trust our experience and our visions"; however, she adds that "we can do neither as long as we internalize the perceptions of reality that have been shaped historically for us by those whose interests fly in our faces."[19] Increasingly, then, the efforts both to reclaim minority history and experience from their shaping by the oppressors and to develop a theology based upon that reclaimed and revalued experience place liberation theology at odds with the "*a priori* presuppositions of tradition."[20] The "elitist mode" of pseudo-objective theologies, shaped by a white, male, heterosexist epistemology, has in fact merely been a way to preserve the power of those who have monopolized theological and religious structures, over against those peoples designated by the elite as "Other." Developing a theology based upon minority experience thus leads the liberation theologian into a tension between personal experience and traditional theological sources and norms.

Feminist theologians have further realized that "the exclusion of our experience from the funding of sacred stories may point to a basic defect in the perception of ultimate power and reality by [those] traditional stories," *rather* than to any putative defectiveness in our experience.[21] Our very exclusion becomes a criticism of scripture and tradition. Revaluing minority experience, therefore, means penetrating and resolving the conflict between experience and tradition by forcibly reopening the "canon." The resultant demand upon gay theology, then, is to search out--to discover and recover--and to further develop our own experience and our own paradigmatic stories. Carter Heyward has begun this process for gay theology when she insists that it is time for gay people to "tell our stories, to listen carefully, to begin to experience our experience, to risk realizing and sharing our own senses of confusion, fear, frustration, anger, even rage, about what is done to us, and what we do to ourselves and others."[22] At one level, that of story in its written, literary form, gay people have long been in the process of capturing and transmitting our particular experience. We do not need to attempt to fit ourselves into, or read ourselves into, heterosexualized experience, history, or tradition, because in the twenty years since the Stonewall Inn riots, gay people have in fact rediscovered a fortuitous wealth of stories ·which reflect the particularities of gay and lesbian history and experience and which depict that experience, not from the oppressor's viewpoint, but from a gay or lesbian point of view.

The process of elucidating and articulating gay and lesbian experience immediately encounters certain limitations, however. As gay people begin to get clear as to what our experience is and is not, we are brought back to the issue of particularity, to the absence of any single, monolithic experience of gay and lesbian being, given our great diversity. We must therefore avoid both universalizing our experience, or so particularizing our experience, in ways which exclude anyone. We must realize the partial, fragmented, and incomplete quality of what we do, both acknowledging our diversity of gender, race, economic class, and life style, while continuing to struggle with concepts which remain unclear for us, such as "gay community"--whom do we mean and whom might we inadvertently be excluding. Fortunately, even starting with the fragments, certain themes and certain historical events emerge from our diversity to provide us with a provisional core of theologizable experience.

To speak of theologically meaningful gay and lesbian history, we must look for in-breaking realities whose impact on gay and lesbian existence radically changed how gay people have lived and experienced their lives. These fragments of gay and lesbian experience have come to include, historically, the various persecutions leading up to and including the gay genocide of Nazism, on the one hand, and our post-Stonewall liberation achievements, on the other hand; personally, the experiences of marginalization and homophobia; and, collectively, the experiences of confronting, responding, mourning, and healing the tragedy of AIDS--of discovering the limits of our mortality, our ability to grieve, and our vast capacity to care for one another in the face of suffering and death. In addition to these fragments of gay and lesbian experience which emerge from the long view, from the sweep of history and contemporary events, other fragments emerge at the developmental or individual level of our experience. Gay theology may also reflect upon the personal experience of self-recognition; the individual struggle to exchange social and familial rejection and sex-negativity for self-affirmation; the risk-taking yet celebratory process of coming out; and, the retrospective reclamation of our personal histories as we infuse our pasts, our childhoods and youths, with gay or lesbian identity, being, and meaning.[23]

* * *

Since I first began collecting and organizing these materials and ideas, I have read Judith Plaskow's and Carol Christ's wonderful new anthology, *Weaving the Visions*.[24] Many of the essays they have included insist even more strongly than previous feminist theology has that our bodiliness and our sexuality are the mediators of our experience and thus, really, of all our knowledge. My own reading of these essays as paradigmatic for gay theology prompts me--by way of a conclusion here--to raise still other questions and issues for our activity of theology. If those of us who are gay men, for example, particularly those of us who deeply identify with the gay ghetto and subculture, are truly going to claim and celebrate our experience as a theological resource, how honest with ourselves are we really willing to be? How much deeper are we willing to delve into our experience and how willing are we to share that experience in the public forum of theological dialogue?

Specifically: Can we acknowledge God's presence in our personal rituals of preparation, whether unconsciously or consciously, for sex--from weight-lifting, exercising, and dieting to grooming and dressing? Is the numinous not pungent in the frenzy of disco music, the sweat of dancing, the smell of poppers, the activities of cruising and pairing up for sex? If indeed, "nothing that is of us can be alien to our theology,"[25] then not only must we *not* be embarrassed by this side of our experience; we must in fact make such an affirmation. Likewise, we must affirm that God was as present in the ooze and smells of the baths before AIDS as he/she is today in the stickiness of non-oxynol-nine lubricants and the snap-tightness of condoms. God is invoked in the flesh on/in flesh of our sexual loving, in the rituals of S/m, and in the archetypal manifestations enhanced by alcohol or drugs. At the same time, however, God is just as present with the sexually or chemically abstinent, with our monogamous couples, with the "worried well," and with the sick; God comforts the lonely while also permeating all the networks of relationships which exist *outside* the ghettoes and bars as well.

God is with us in safe sex and in our grief at AIDS, with us in the job opportunities lost to homophobia and in the despair of broken relationships, as well as in our struggles to come out, to accept ourselves, to nurture self-esteem, to build community, and in our efforts to forgive both our ex-lovers and our friends lost to AIDS for abandoning us ... as well as in our efforts, also, to forgive ourselves for surviving. The divine is intimately interwoven in our passions—whether for justice or for our lovers' bodies—in the nitty-gritty of our sexuality, in our tears and our caring in the midst of AIDS, in our political battles, in all the mundaneness of our daily activities as well as in the campy humor and drama of our lives, in gay pride and self-pride, and in the passionate renewal of love—in the mixture of the silly giggles and the reclaimed and redefined masculinity we gay men can discover in embracing a brother/lover/friend! God permeates every parcel of our experience, our being and doing, and lifts those up—as something sacred—on a strong and tender cosmic embrace. So held up and held together in community by that empowering embrace, here together, is where our theologizing must begin!

―――――[1]Malcolm Boyd, "Telling a lie for Christ?," *Gay spirit: Myth & meaning* (M. Thompson, ed.; New York: St. Martin's Press, 1987), p. 79.

[2]Rosemary Radford Ruether, *To change the world: Christology & cultural criticism* (New York: Crossroad/Continuum, 1983), p. 5.

[3]George R. Edwards, *Gay/lesbian liberation: A biblical perspective* (New York: Pilgrim Press, 1984), pp. 88-89.

[4]Ruether, p. 27.

[5]cf., John E. Fortunato, *Embracing the exile: Healing journeys of gay Christians* (New York: Seabury Press, 1983).

[6]I. Carter Heyward, *The redemption of God: A theology of mutual relation* (Washington: University Press of America), p. 20.

[7]Richard L. Rubenstein, *After Auschwitz: Radical theology & contemporary Judaism* (Indianapolis: Bobbs-Merrill, 1966), p. 246.

[8]I. Carter Heyward, *Our passion for justice: Images of power, sexuality, & liberation* (New York: Pilgrim Press, 1984), p. 225.

[9]Rubenstein, p. 246.

[10]Heyward, *Our passion*, pp. 223-224.

[11]Carol P. Christ & Judith Plaskow, "Introduction[s]," *Womanspirit rising: A feminist reader in religion* (C. P. Christ & J. Plaskow, eds.; San Francisco: Harper & Row, 1979), p. 20.

[12]Rosemary Radford Ruether, *Sexism & God-talk: Toward a feminist theology* (Boston: Beacon Press, 1983), p. 18.

[13]Boyd, p. 84.

[14]Ruether, *Sexism*, p. 20.

[15]Heyward, *Our passion*, p. 68.

[16]J. Michael Clark, "AIDS, death, & God: Gay liberational theology and the problem of suffering," *Journal of Pastoral Counseling* 21.1 (Spring-Summer 1986), pp. 40-54.

[17]Heyward, *Our passion*, p. 7.

[18]Sheila D. Collins, "Theology in the politics of Appalachian women," *Womanspirit rising: A feminist reader in religion* (C. P. Christ & J. Plaskow, eds.; San Francisco: Harper & Row, 1979), p. 152, emphasis added.

[19]Heyward, *Our passion*, pp. 7, 158.

[20]Sheila D. Collins, "Feminist theology at the crossroads," *Christianity & Crisis* 41.20 (14 December 1981), p. 343.

[21]Carol P. Christ, "Spiritual quest and women's experience," *Womanspirit rising: A feminist reader in religion* (C. P. Christ & J. Plaskow, eds.; San Francisco: Harper & Row, 1979), p. 230.

[22]Heyward, *Our passion*, p. 85.

[23]cf., Al Cotton, "Backtracking," *Amethyst* 1.1 (Spring 1987), pp. 44-45.

[24]Judith Plaskow & Carol P. Christ (eds.), *Weaving the visions: New patterns in feminist spirituality* (San Francisco: Harper & Row, 1989).

[25]cf., note 18, above.

IV. E. Michael Gorman

A Special Window: An Anthropological Perspective on Spirituality in Contemporary U.S. Gay Male Culture [1]

The following are preliminary reflections about gay (male) American culture and aspects of the spirituality of that subculture from an anthropologist's point of view. "Spirituality" herein reflects informants' use of the term, as an emic category which has emerged as a recognized aspect of gay life in the U.S. It encompasses such notions as, "a connection with one's inner self connected to a larger consciousness," "being the truth that I know, and not hiding," "a movement toward wholeness, to live values around authenticity"; it refers to "our experience of the spirit and our place in the universe"; "it is our experience of God."

Because religion and spirituality are intrinsically related to other aspects of culture, their explication must *a priori* begin with looking at the social and historical contexts of the gay subculture. Beginning with some personal

background and a few comments on anthropological methodologies used, I will therefore
discuss what I call the core symbols, rituals,
and cultural performances which are salient in
the contemporary gay male world, as it has
emerged in the post-Stonewall (post-1969) era,
on into the age of AIDS. I use "cultural per-
formance" in the sense that Milton Singer does,
as an important event or ritual of a culture that
contains within itself distillations of key symbols, themes, patterns, and values of that culture.[2] Two primary complexes of events--*kairetic* events in the sense of *kairos* or critical
time--have served, then, to infuse, color, and
mark with special poignancy the experiences
gay men have of God. These events are **(1)** the
rite of passage which is *coming out* as a gay
person, both individually and socially, and **(2)**
the impact of the AIDS health crisis.

    While my work has primarily been epi-
demiological and health policy related--from
1986 until 1990 in Los Angeles--I have nevertheless been struck by the number of situations
in which issues of spirituality or religion arose,
by the number of times an informant used religious language to describe a personal experience, and by the sheer number of overtly spiritual, metaphysical, or religious organizations
which have emerged over the last 5-7 years.
Doubtless, some have to do with the aging of
the community and with the aging of that particular group of gay men who constitute the
"Stonewall cohort," gay men who came out in

the late 1960s and early 1970s. Some of these developments have also coincided with the AIDS crisis, and yet they are not *simply* related to AIDS, however much this crisis may serve as a catalyst. For the first time since I have been involved in the study of the life of this community, spirituality has finally "come out of the closet"; there has been an awakening of interest in things of the spirit broadly defined.

Interesting as this sociological observation might be, of even greater importance has been the articulation of that which provided historical and cultural context for this to occur, i.e., the cultural ground for the experience of God particular to gay men. If the language which dialectical theologians used to talk about their experience of God was drawn from their experience of WWI battlefields, then the language gay men use to describe God is, appropriately, the language of the experience of coming out and living in the gay world, along with the concomitant experience of oppression, and the experience of the AIDS crisis. One way to clarify this issue is to frame it in anthropological terms. Consequently, I use the words of my informants, my own participation in and observation of the daily life of the community and its organizations, rituals, and cultural performances as a kind of (con)text upon which to reflect on its overall meaning, i.e., the cultural ground of gay religious experience and spirituality.

Herein, I am not interested in delineating stages, nor for that matter with clarifying psychological processes, so much as I am interested in looking at the sociocultural processes and the ethos of gay (male) life and examining how these relate to and inform religious experience. Clifford Geertz describes "ethos" as the "tone, character, and quality of people's life, their moral and aesthetic style, their underlying attitude toward themselves and their world."[3] Social structural processes are those aspects of culture that relate to the collective life of a community and which are intrinsic to the creation and sustenance of a community--its history, ritual, rites of passage, institutions, and code of conduct.

Anthropologists traditionally use a variety of methodologies when undertaking fieldwork. Chief among these are participant observation or immersion into the culture, interviews, both unstructured and semi-structured, and various other modes of observation, including unobtrusive and reactive observation. Archival research is involved as well. All of these strategies were used in gathering data for this project, and in a number of different kinds of settings from churches, bars, clubs, and organizations to major community events such as gay/lesbian pride celebrations and the October 1987 March on Washington.

What is meant by gay (male) culture and whether it even exists has been feverishly debated: I contend that gay culture is consti-

tuted by a particular set of symbols and meanings, and by a code for conduct. It is, however,
a relatively recent historical phenomenon
whose direct roots go back approximately sixty
years, but which has particularly emerged over
the last twenty years. While the notion of "gay
symbols" may be arguable, there is in fact a
universe of artifacts, signs, institutions, and
sensibilities that constitute such a symbolic
universe. Some historical symbols of gay culture are the pink triangle, the rainbow flag,
Harvey Milk, San Francisco and the Stonewall
Inn Riots, which story itself attains mythic
character. Related to these symbols, both en-
capsulating and concretizing them as part of
the culture, are the rituals and social processes
intrinsic to the constellation of the gay world.
These rituals and processes include coming
out, gay pride parades, political demonstra-
tions, and the establishment of gay identified
territorial communities or "ghettoes." The
AIDS crisis has also introduced a new array of
symbols, rituals, and processes into the gay
(male) symbolic universe.

Among the pre-AIDS symbols, the pink
triangle is one of the most powerful and ubi-
quitous. Originally a mark of terrible stigma
and humiliating death, the pink triangle was
worn by gays sent to their death in the level
three Nazi concentration camps during WWII.
As part of the gay liberation movement, the
triangle has been transformed into a symbol of
pride and triumph over oppression. The rain-

bow flag, originally designed in the mid-1970s for a San Francisco Gay Freedom Day parade whose theme was "Over the Rainbow," is another more recent symbol which represents the multi-layered diversity of the gay community.

Harvey Milk represents a different kind of symbol, a cultural hero, a prophet in the literal sense of "one who speaks for others." As an early, openly gay elected public official, Milk came to serve as a role model for gay people, representing a new kind of power in his participation in government as an openly gay man. His murder--for gay people, his martyrdom--represents a tragic and premature end to his spreading the good news of liberation, on par with the martyrdom of Oscar Romero in El Salvador some years later. Milk's martyrdom served to solidify the community and to call others to undertake the task as well.

San Francisco also assumes symbolic qualities as the preeminent gay political and cultural center of the nation. It is no accident that Milk came out of San Francisco, that the city generated the first gay rights laws, that the foremost AIDS prevention and treatment models were developed there, or that the idea for the AIDS memorial quilt (the Names Project) originated there. San Francisco represents the emotional and spiritual heart of the gay symbolic universe; Castro and 18th streets represent the pivot of the four corners for gay people and, in that sense, the city is *the* "city on

the hill"--the *new Jerusalem* and a place of pil-
grimage.
    The June 1969 Stonewall Riots in New
York City represent a particularly paradigmatic *kairetic* event in gay history; for the first
time--at least as widely reported--gay people
fought police harassment. The event quickly
achieved mythic status and constituted a very
critical symbolic watershed in gay/lesbian
history. Twenty years later, gay pride parades
and festivals around the world celebrate the
Stonewall Riots. Stonewall serves as a *myth of
origins* for the beginnings of the gay political
movement. In the same way that for Ameri-
cans the Boston Tea Party and the events at
Lexington and Concord were catalysts for the
American revolution, so the riot of drag queens
and others at the Stonewall Inn has assumed a
reality larger than the events themselves.
Stonewall also constitutes a myth in the sense
that it mediates, or articulates, fundamental
contradictions within the subculture. The idea
of drag queens fighting the macho, powerful
New York police confounds basic assumptions
about gay men and how they should behave.
In the old order they would have accepted harassment and arrest in shame; in the new order, they fought back, became models for a different kind of behavior, and typified a new
consciousness about the essence of being gay--
pride vs. contempt, liberation vs. oppression.
    Also related to the gay symbolic uni-
verse are those processes, rituals, and institu-

tions which constitute the gay world. Among the most central is that of the coming out process. In *A New Light on Zion,* I described coming out in these terms:

> ...A change of status occurred in coming out as a gay man or [lesbian], the individual having previously perceived himself/herself as either "straight" or as a "closet" homosexual.
>
> Coming out entails ... participation in a gay collectivity and a gay social identity. Gayness is constituted by a set of symbols and meanings and a code of conduct ... the concomitant significant feature of which is the coming out process during which one *becomes* gay, comes to an understanding of gay symbols and gay ideology, identifies with them and becomes oriented to the sensibilities of gay life. One comes to an acceptance which is a new perception of one's self. With regard to collective identity one defines oneself with respect to one's boundaries or in terms of differentiation from heterosexuals ... and with respect to the commonalities and bonds one shares with gay [people] in terms of affiliation.[4]

During this fieldwork several informants also expressed the centrality of this event in their lives: "To me, discovering and figuring out that I was gay was a great relief. ...It took me some months to start going out and meeting people; one of the first things I did was to call up friends and tell them I was gay. It was a great weight lifted off my shoulders."[5]

Once "out of the closet," individuals usually began to celebrate their gayness and to reach out to other gay people. The establishment of territorial communities was an important part of this process and the first decade after Stonewall saw a plethora of gay ghettoes established in virtually every major U.S. city. These were modeled after San Francisco's Castro, New York's West Village, or Los Angeles' West Hollywood and Silverlake. Although in some cities these "bohemian" districts had existed for years, the 1970s saw them develop dramatically into cohesive urban communities, as described elsewhere.[6] In these settings a variety of organizations, businesses, clubs, restaurants, and churches became established which catered to the needs of the newly formed enclaves. The populations of these neighborhoods also grew dramatically as new migrants poured in to escape the difficulty of life in the heartland or the expectations of families of origin. Senses of exile and loss accompanied this movement away from home, because the gay newcomers could not be who they were there, and yet a greater sense of relief also permeated these new communities, mixed with a tremendous exhilaration as the newcomers experimented with new ways of living, established new homes and lives for themselves, and celebrated their newfound freedom to be gay--like pilgrims in a new land.

With the establishment of new communities also came political awareness and the beginnings of participation in the political process as openly gay people. Harvey Milk was one of the first, but he was soon followed by a number of others.[7] By the early 1980s gays were thought to constitute nearly 20% of San Francisco's electorate and they had considerable political clout in a number of other cities as well. The gay pride parades became vehicles for expressing cultural values and for articulating the community's political agenda--decriminalization of sodomy statutes, the extension and protection of gay/lesbian civil rights--as well as showplaces for the organizational strength and diversity of the gay community. By the late 1970s these parades and festivals drew hundreds of thousands in major cities.

If the 1970s were a watershed politically and culturally for the gay community, the 1980s were marked by an entirely different leitmotif--the AIDS crisis. From the first terse CDC announcement in June 1981 of the deaths of five young gay men due to a mysterious immunosuppressive illness, to the present time in which over 50,000 gay men have died, the AIDS crisis has exacted a staggering toll that will continue well into the next decade. Even with AIDS becoming more like a chronic disease, the HIV virus will rob years of life from those infected. This does not even begin to account for the emotional, financial, or social toll which extends far beyond the gay community.

One informant summed it up as, "AIDS is like a war." Another man said, "You never know who is going next. Who can you depend on? Which friend is going to leave? Will I be one of the survivors?"

Every bit as much as the Stonewall decade, the initial AIDS decade has etched its mark upon gay (male) culture and transformed it. It has been a catalyst for remarkably quick health and sexual behavior changes on a scale not heretofore imagined, and yet it remains an abiding presence of things eschatological, of still-mobilizing resources--an ever present reality. One important symbol that has become a significant addition to the gay universe is the Names Project AIDS memorial quilt; other AIDS rituals have also become commonplace, including AIDS-related healing services sponsored by various organizations, churches, and programs; volunteerism and caregiving through a variety of AIDS service organizations; and, rituals related to mourning and grief. The needs of the health crisis have been superimposed on the gay pride parades and, in many of these events in the late 1980s, the largest groups marching were AIDS services volunteers. Political activism has also been bolstered by the need to press continually for more public funds for prevention, treatment, and research. Also, a new generation and style of gay social justice-seeking has been visited upon local and federal governments under the aegis of the *AIDS Coalition to Unleash Power*, or ACT-UP. Gay political activism likewise reached a new pinnacle in the 1987 March on Washington.

The Names Project AIDS memorial quilt represents a poignant and riveting image at once beautiful and sorrowful. The picture of 100,000+ people milling about and weeping over the quilt--during its three displays in Washington (1987, 1988, 1989) as well as in all the other cities where portions of the quilt have visited--as if it were a battleground, was starkly powerful. The quilt is painful to gaze upon in part because it conjures up emotions of loss, sorrow, disbelief, anger, and neglect, if not social and political betrayal. Yet, for gay people and all those impacted by the AIDS crisis, gay and nongay, the quilt has also come to symbolize permanence and a legitimation of all the lives of those felled by the virus, people who might otherwise go unnamed and unremembered. The quilt is a forceful symbol of determined resistance to attempts to silence the reality of the health crisis and, by extension, gayness, and to make of it and those risk groups most directly impacted by it, a shameful secret and yet another stigma.

The quilt symbolizes a triumph for those gay and nongay people who created it, an instance of turning an occasion of oppression and grief into an enduring and positive memorial. The quilt for gay people is something holy--a Torah, a shroud, a monument to truth and authenticity and love. The needs of the health crisis have similarly transformed the landscape of gay territorial communities. While dozens of sexually oriented establishments such as the bathhouses have closed, a myriad of AIDS service organizations have opened to care for the sick and the dying. The community has been called to serve and thousands have volunteered, in terms of both service hours and money. Another ritual process that has transformed the community has been the process of mourning associated with AIDS.

One might now ask: "How do these symbols, myths, rituals, and performances function? What do they mean? How do they relate to the experience of God?" They do so in three ways.

In the first case, underlying all these symbols, myths, and rituals is a salient hallmark, a message. Or, to use a theological term, *kerygma*. The bottom line, the germ of that message, is that "gay is good," and gay existence is borne out of a context and structure of oppression which must be acknowledged. To be gay is to have to struggle to live one's life with authenticity--and that is not easy. As with any religious symbol, these are not intrinsically easy or happy or especially hopeful symbols on their own. On the contrary, they are difficult and painful--we do not contemplate the reality of the pink triangle or the quilt easily. Yet, they are transformed into symbols of hope and triumph and joy by the message; indeed, they constitute part of the message. They tell us that we, too, are free--if we accept ourselves and our freedom. They tell us that we can overcome, that we shall be named, that we shall be acknowledged for who we are. They give us hope. And, they tell us that we must come to that place in our lives as pilgrims seeking the truth within us.

A second theme in these cultural artifacts, processes, and performances is community, or in theological language, *koinonia.* This theme or value is expressed concretely in the establishment of territorial communities, however imperfectly. For the first time in history these communities dare to say in a number of ways, "gay people are a people;" "we are a we" and as such have common needs, shared meanings, and collective hopes for, a vision about, our future. This is not to say that we all have exactly the same parameters for that vision, or see it in the same light. The fact is that we can talk about ourselves and look back to our past individually *and* collectively as well as look to whatever the future may bring, as a people on the way. Not only are we *not* sinful or sick, but we celebrate ourselves as a community, especially during gay pride, but also at many other times as well. We have also gone out from our community and recognized our bonds with others. The AIDS crisis has been a catalyst for this process. We can recognize that we are like other people even if they are not gay and, thus, we have begun to appreciate our shared woundedness with them, the commonalities of our structures of oppression. In this sense we acknowledge that an important part of our message is that we are all part of a larger community of the stigmatized. We are still grappling with this issue in some fundamental ways, but a *conscienticization* process is occurring.

The third theme, particularly in the context of AIDS, is service, or *diakonia.* If the AIDS health crisis has pounded us with loss and grief, it has also called forth our abilities to give compassion and to be of service to the sick and the dying. It is in being of service that we actualize the message of liberation and the experience of community.

Entering the 1990s we find ourselves at a very important juncture in our cultural evolution as gay men and as such it is appropriate for us to reflect on the meanings, methods, and prospects with regard to a constructive gay theology, and how it is we discover God in the gayness of our daily lives. This process of characterizing, defining, and distinguishing the landscape of our God-experience will be all the richer if it draws on a variety of methodologies, perspectives, and views of gay life. In an interview with Mark Thompson several years ago, Harry Hay said,

> ...All of us grew up knowing we had a
> secret in ourselves that was different from other

people. ...Regardless of what we heard--that it was dirty, it was bad, it was against God--we somehow knew it was beautiful and good. We didn't know how to express it, but we had faith that someday we would. Then that wonderful day comes when you find that you're not alone, that there are others like you. You begin to fantasize that there is going to be that one who understands you and has gone through the same things. And the day will come when you'll take his or her hand and understand and share everything perfectly. ...Gays have a special window, our own way of seeing, our own vision.[8]

Acknowledging and articulating and sharing the specialness of our vision with each other together constitute our shared tasks as theologians. Our faith has not been in vain and it gives us hope for the future.

------

[1]Because the author's final, submitted version of this essay did not conform to the series style-sheet, the *editors* have further revised it appropriately, for style and active voice, to include it in the present volume.

[2]Milton Singer, "The cultural pattern of Indian civilization," *Far East. Qtrly.*, 15(1955):23-36.

[3]Clifford Geertz, *The interpretation of cultures* (New York: Basic Bks., 1972).

[4]E.M. Gorman, *A new light on Zion*, Ph.D. Diss., Univ. Chicago, 1980, p. 6.

[5]*Ibid.*, p. 122.

[6]cf., E.M. Gorman, "Introduction: Anthropology and AIDS," *Med. Anthro. Qtrly.,* 17(1986):31-32, and, "The AIDS epidemic in San Francisco: Epidemiological and anthropological perspectives," *Anthropology and epidemiology* (eds., C.R. Jones, R. Stall, S.M. Gifford; Dordrecht: D. Reidel, 1986), pp. 157-172.

[7]Elaine Noble of Massachusetts was *the* first elected official openly identified with the gay/lesbian community.

[8]Mark Thompson, "Harry Hay: A voice from the past, a vision for the future," *Gay spirit: Myth and meaning* (ed., M. Thompson; New York: St. Martin's Pr., 1987), pp. 182-199.

V. John J. McNeill

Response

It is a real pleasure to be the respondent to these three presentations dealing with gay men's issues in religion, especially since all three are of exceptional quality. In light of the recent murder of Ignacio Ellacuria and his companions because of their work in the field of *third world* liberation theology, I am also intensely aware of the courage of these three men to enter the field of *gay/lesbian* liberation theology. ...And I am also sure that all three presenters have already experienced some persecution in academia because of their audacity.[1]

The first observation I would like to make of all three papers, especially Clark's and Thurston's, is the good use they make of other liberation theologies in constructing a theology of gay/lesbian liberation. Feminist liberation thinkers as well as third world liberationists and Black liberationists have already done much of the preliminary work for us in terms of methodology and procedure. An adequate undertaking of gay/lesbian liberation theology demands that one be deeply immersed in liberation theology in all its forms. Thurston makes use of James Cone, Juan Luis Segundo, and Gustavo Gutierrez, while Clark makes use of Carol Christ and Judith Plaskow, Carter Heyward, Richard Rubenstein, Rosemary Radford Ruether, and Ellen Umansky.

However, I feel that none of the papers dealt adequately with the fundamental *differences* between gay/lesbian liberation theology and the other forms. In my view, the essential difference is the fact that for centuries there has been no visible community of gay men and lesbians. Women are born into a community of women; Blacks are born into a community of Blacks; the poor are usually born into a community of the poor. But, gay men and lesbians are born into a heterosexual family community and, at least in the past, were initially unaware of any other persons like themselves. Becoming a part of a gay/lesbian *community* is, therefore, a conscious choice and involves the often very painful act of coming out of the closet....

The second primary difference is the fact that only gay men and lesbians grow up with the message that what they are was/is morally evil. To use the words of the Vatican, gayness is "an intrinsic orientation toward evil." The result has been that most gays/lesbians from a religious family background grew up seeing themselves as "defective creations" and God as a sadistic god. This has lead many gay men and lesbians into deep psychological woundedness and interiorized homophobia, which gets reconfirmed with every contact with the church and our culture.

There is an extraordinary need, as a result, for a healing community in which gay men and lesbians can learn self-acceptance and a healthy sense of gay/lesbian pride. All three papers make excellent contributions on the level of scholarship to the formation of such a community. I am intensely aware, after twenty years of pastoral work, that gay people can be and often are their own worst enemies, acting out their internalized homophobia in a syndrome of self-hate, cynicism, and mutual sadism--in a fashion exemplified in the film, *The Boys in the Band*. To do successful work in this community, therefore, calls for extraordinary self-analysis, maturity, and mental health.

Related to this concern, I would like to make a general observation about graduate studies dealing with gay/lesbian liberation. From my own experience teaching graduate students, I find that many people and especially gay people use what we in psychotherapy call the "intellectual defense." Emotional development is frequently so blocked that the individual tries to handle life exclusively with the mind. This can lead to an extraordinary development of mental abilities, but underlying that brilliance is an emotional immaturity which can lead to an extremely destructive use of intellectual powers divorced from a search for truth. There is also a serious danger to the individual scholar who in a crisis could experience burn-out or psychological break-down.

I highly recommend that anyone involved in research and scholarship, especially in the area of gay/lesbian liberation, also be involved in both individual and group psychotherapy (I am of the opinion that this should be a universal requirement of all graduate schools and not just for the students!). Being involved as a gay man in gay/lesbian liberation is not just a head trip, but a heart trip as well. Consequently, it is wise to get into therapy and work out any residual problems one may have with his/her gay or lesbian identity--before these get acted out transferentially with colleagues in academia.

All three papers agree that the starting point for gay/lesbian liberation theology has to be just this consolidarity with the experience of gay people. Thurston, making use of Segundo's understanding of the hermeneutic circle, believes that the only way to approach scripture in a liberating way is to begin with gay/lesbian experience. We must assume the legitimacy of gay/lesbian experience and show the world that the gay/lesbian struggle is a legitimate dimension of the gospels. Clark similarly speaks of reclaiming subjectivity as a theological resource, in critical tension with traditionally homophobic scriptural and doctrinal norms and givens. And, Gorman brings to his presentation on anthropological issues the wealth of his own background working with AIDS as an epidemiologist.

An implication of all three papers, one which none of them spells out *explicitly,* is that the only one who can legitimately make a contribution to gay/lesbian liberation theology is someone who is both gay/lesbian and "out of the closet." The problem here has some similarity to the question, "Can a gay man (or lesbian) do therapy with any other than a gay (or lesbian) therapist?" I would like to see an explicit wrestling with the implications of this.

I totally disagree with a statement concerning my own work in Thurston's essay. He essentially says that "within the revisionist camp, McNeill does not realize that his suspicions arise from a new way of experiencing the world. Anachronistically he projects contemporary experience back into Christian origins, imposing the category of sexual orientation on ancient texts."[2] First of all, I very explicitly make the point that the authors of scripture were unaware of what we understand today as homosexual orientation, but dealt exclusively with sexual behavior.[3] The second point I made was that it was homophobic translators who read the word "homosexual" back into the texts. I saw as my primary task in this book to try to restore the original meaning of the texts, by removing the layers of homophobic translation and interpretation that had distorted them.

Likewise, I also resist the simplistic handing over of the biblical texts to our "enemies" which I detect in these papers. Clark speaks contemptuously of apologetic efforts to justify gay/lesbian existence with biblical exegesis as functioning merely "to diffuse our efforts, keeping us [passively] waiting ... for a positive response which is unlikely ever to come."[4] We are still waiting for the definitive critical scriptural study of homosexuality, but there is already adequate scholarly grounds to make the statement that nowhere in scripture is there a *universal* condemnation of same sex activity. We must take the total silence of the four gospels on this issue seriously. However, the presenters are absolutely correct when they make the point that any challenge to the mainline churches and traditions should not come from a need to be accepted and validated by others. If we do so, we have forfeited the possibility of liberation.

I fully agree with all three papers that the primary source of gay/lesbian liberation theology has to be the collective subjective experience of gay people. In fact, in my most recent book,[5] I quote Thomas Clarke, S.J., that the only way to do theology in general today is to begin with "revelatory experience": My intention in that book is to provide a spirituality based in the revelatory experience of gay and lesbian Christians. Surprisingly, none of the papers mentioned this text and one explicitly denied my use of this methodology.

The very fact that we base our efforts on the uniqueness of the subjective experience of gay people would seem to imply that we have taken a position in the major controversy concerning homosexuality today--the essentialist vs. the constructionist schools. Interestingly, none of the papers dealt with this controversy and/or its implications for gay/lesbian liberation theology. I myself think that the very idea of a gay/lesbian identity which could be the foundation for a theology necessarily puts us on the essentialist side of this controversy.

I would like to see a better use made of the traditional positions that justify the use of subjective experience as a theological resource. For example, the traditional belief in freedom of conscience is based on the belief that God speaks to every individual directly in his/her heart and one has the right to formulate behavior by a "discernment of spirits"--i.e., by listening carefully to what God is saying to us through our direct experience.

I fully agree with Clark that God is present in and through healthy human sexuality, both heterosexual and homosexual. Gay men and lesbians have made a special contribution to integrating sexuality with spirituality. I have serious reservations, however, about his *im*plicit pantheistic celebration of God's presence in each and every manifestation of gay/lesbian sexuality, regardless of that sexual activity's relationship or lack of relationship to human intimacy and personal love.

I am too much the psychotherapist to be completely comfortable with the assumption that God is equally present in any and every expression of sexuality, from S/m to using poppers on the dance floor, for example. I do agree that gay men and lesbians must work out their own sexual ethics based on their own experience.[6] But I am also aware that psychopathology underlies much sexual activity, both gay and straight. For example, compulsive, self-centered "sexaholism" is, I believe, incompatible with the total "presence of God." If Iraneus was correct and "the glory of God is humans fully alive," then those expressions of human sexuality which do not render humans fully alive do not have a fullness of the sacramental dimension. The gay/lesbian community has a desperate need for the means to discern between healthy and pathological sexuality. In my practice as a psychotherapist, I am aware that pathological sexuality usually springs from and confirms self-hatred.

One last point--I was deeply impressed by the use Gorman made of the Names Project quilt (the AIDS memorial) as a symbol of the special outlook on life and death found in the gay/lesbian community. Among the meanings he discusses, he says, "The quilt is a forceful symbol of determined resistance to attempts to silence the reality of the health crisis and, by extension, gayness, and to make of AIDS and those risk groups most directly impacted by it, a shameful secret and yet another stigma."[7]

Gorman's words stimulated me to think of several other aspects of the quilt that reflect a different attitude in the gay/lesbian community to life, death, and other values.

In contrast to the typical graveyard memorial which is usually monumental and designed to last for centuries (e.g., the Vietnam Memorial), the quilt is something delicate, perishable, and both aesthetically beautiful and totally personal. It makes its appearance--it is brought out of the closet--at selected times and places as *a deliberate choice* and then is returned again to the closet. Again, in contrast to the depersonalization of most memorials, each panel of the quilt remembers in a unique and special way the personality of the one being remembered and celebrates the personal love that was given and received by that individual.

Finally, I would like to offer two last, related questions which these papers do not address. Why is gay/lesbian liberation in general and gay/lesbian liberation theology (and spirituality) almost exclusively pursued in North America?[8] And, how can we begin to *export* our gay/lesbian contribution to liberation theology (and spirituality)? With these questions and my critical suggestions here, I wish to stimulate all of us to continue the work courageously begun with such promise here.

---

[1]It is worth noting that all three presenters during the 1989 meetings of the Gay Men's Issues in Reli-

gion Consultation of the American Academy of Religion were in fact, "unaffiliated scholars." None of them held a traditional academic appointment [editors' note].

[2]cf., p. 16, above [editors' note].

[3]J.J. McNeill, *The church and the homosexual* (Boston: Beacon Press, 1988, rev. ed.), pp. 38-42.

[4]cf., p. 27, above [editors' note].

[5]J.J. McNeill, *Taking a chance on God: Liberating theology for gays, lesbians, their lovers, families, and friends* (Boston: Beacon Press, 1988).

[6]cf., for example, the since published text: J.M. Clark, *A defiant celebration: Theological ethics and gay sexuality* (Garland, TX: Tangelwüld Press, 1990) [editors' note].

[7]cf., p. 56, above [editors' note].

[8]Noteworthy exceptions will be studied during the 1990 annual meeting of the Gay Men's Issues in Religion Group and will be published as the third volume in the Gay Men's Issues in Religious Studies series [editors' note].

VI. Notes on Contributors

J. Michael Clark, M.Div., Ph.D., is currently co-chair of the Gay Men's Issues in Religion Group of the American Academy of Religion and is both an "independent scholar" & a part-time instructor in the Freshmen English Program of Georgia State University (Atlanta). He is the author of *A Place to Start: Toward an Unapologetic Gay Liberation Theology* (Dallas: Monument Press, 1989)--from which this essay is excerpted; *A Defiant Celebration: Theological Ethics and Gay Sexuality* (Garland, TX: Tangelwüld Press, 1990); & *A Lavender Cosmic Pilgrim: Further Ruminations on Gay Spirituality, Theology, and Sexuality* (Las Colinas, TX: The Liberal Press, 1990).

E. Michael Gorman, Ph.D., is an anthropologist and an epidemiologist with a background in religion and philosophy. His dissertation, entitled *A New Light on Zion*, examined the cultural construction of gay/lesbian identity using fieldwork in three gay/lesbian religious congregations in Chicago in the late 1970s. Since 1981 he has worked in various aspects of the HIV epidemic as an epidemiologist, a health education and prevention specialist, and as a health policy analyst in San Francisco (Univ. Calif., SF), in Atlanta (CDC), and in Los Angeles (Rand Health Sci. Prog.). He is currently

Program Director for the California HIV Planning Project at the Western Consortium for Public Health (Berkeley) and a lecturer at the School of Public Health (Univ. Calif., Berkeley).

John J. McNeill is the author of *The Church and the Homosexual* (Kansas City: Sheed, Andrews & McMeel, 1976, rev. & exp. ed., Boston: Beacon Press, 1988) & *Taking a Chance on God: Liberating Theology for Gays, Lesbians, their Lovers, Families, and Friends* (Boston: Beacon Press, 1988). He was the guest respondent of the Gay Men's Issues in Religion Consultation of the American Academy of Religion during its 1989 meeting in Anaheim.

Michael L. Stemmeler, Dipl. Theol., M.A., Ph.D., is currently co-chair of the Gay Men's Issues in Religion Group of the American Academy of Religion and an assistant professor of religion at Central Michigan University. As leading co-editor of this series, he is the author of "Gays--A Threat to Society? Social Policy in Nazi Germany and the Aftermath," in *Homophobia & the Judaeo-Christian Tradition* (series volume 1; Dallas: Monument Press, 1990), pp. 69-93.

Thomas M. Thurston, Ph.D., is currently negotiating for the publication of his recently completed text, *A Gay Theology of Liberation,* from which this essay is excerpted. An "independent scholar" in San Francisco, his current projects include an article, "Natural Relations: A Response to Richard B. Hays' Hermeneutics of Romans I," and a second book, *Gay Weddings.*

Index, 75